MW01078012

BarbraStreisand

text **Patricia Mulrooney Eldred**
illustrations **John Keely**
design concept **Mark Landkamer**

published by **Creative Education**
Mankato, Minnesota

Published by Creative Educational Society, Inc.,
123 South Broad Street, Mankato, Minnesota 56001
Copyright © 1975 by Creative Educational Society, Inc. International
copyrights reserved in all countries.
No part of this book may be reproduced in any form without written permission
from the publisher. Printed in the United States.
Distributed by Childrens Press, 1224 West Van Buren Street, Chicago, Illinois 60607
Library of Congress Numbers: 75-20385   ISBN 0-87191-459-X
Library of Congress Cataloging in Publication Data
Eldred, Patricia Mulrooney.
Barbra Streisand.
SUMMARY: A brief biography concentrating on the career of the
well-known singer and movie star.
Bibliography: p.
1. Streisand, Barbra—Juvenile literature.
[1. Streisand, Barbra.   2. Singers]   I. Keely, John.   II. Title.
ML3930.S88E4   790.2'092'4   [B]   [92]   75-20385   ISBN 0-87191-459-X

On a summer night in Brooklyn, New York, a small girl sat alone on the roof of a six-story brick apartment building. As she watched the night sky, she dreamed what seemed to be an impossible dream . . . that someday she would be a famous star.

The Star

The dream was not impossible. Fifteen years later, on another summer night in another part of New York City, the same girl watched the night sky. But this time she was not alone. She was surrounded by 135,000 people who had come to hear her sing.

For two and a half hours Barbra Streisand entertained a huge and enthusiastic audience in a style that has come to be totally her own.

She was funny. The audience applauded her entrance; and she responded, in her Brooklyn accent, "I didn't do nothin' yet."

Barbra was dressed in a characteristically unusual outfit — a pink pleated gown under a pink chiffon cape. Critic Rex Reed later described the dress as "a cut up parachute dyed in Rit."

Barbra was singing in the style her fans loved. There were the old favorites, "Cry Me a River" and "People." There were new songs, "Natural Sounds" and "New Love Is Like a Newborn Child." In response to all of them, the audience — the largest ever assembled to see one entertainer perform — cheered, applauded, and shouted for more.

At one point in the concert Barbra paused while all applause and noise died, and a hush settled over the crowd. She spoke quietly but intensely. "We're all very lucky, I think, that the night was so lovely. Last night it was *so* humid, but tonight is very, sort of, in a strange way, peaceful." And then, slowly and movingly on a June night, she sang a traditional Christmas song, "Silent Night."

It was 1967. Her concert, "A Happening in Central Park," was a dream come true for Barbra. She was a star.

The Dreamer

Barbra's memories of her childhood dreaming days are mostly depressing ones. She has remarked, "We weren't *poor,* poor; but we didn't have anything."

She was born April 24, 1942, in Brooklyn, New York. Her father, a teacher of English and psychology, died when she was fifteen months old.

Although she was only a young child, this event continued to affect Barbra's life. She commented later, "When a kid grows up missing one parent, there's a big gap that has to be filled. It's like someone being blind; they hear better. With me, I felt more, I sensed more, I wanted more . . ."

For sensitive Barbra, the early years of her life were lonely. Her mother worked to support the family. Her brother Sheldon was eight years older than Barbra and not interested in being her companion.

Barbra never felt she was a real part of her family. She once told a reporter that she used to ask, "O.K., Ma, did you find me on a door step or what?"

She rejected much of the Orthodox Jewish tradition which surrounded her. She recalls that she wasn't supposed to say the word "Christmas" while the Rabbi was visiting; but as soon as he left their apartment, she would repeat the word over and over.

Other children noticed that Barbra was shy and awkward. They teased her about her nose, calling her "big beak" and taunting her with "crazy Barbara."

8

Because she was lonely and dissatisfied, Barbra began experimenting with methods of escape from her unhappy world.

She looked forward to Saturday afternoons when she could sit in the local movie theater and totally lose herself in the lives of the characters on the screen. Then she could forget the dreariness of the Brooklyn streets, the dullness of the apartment, the ridicule of the other children. She was transported to a fantasy world where people were beautiful, happy, and loved. As she later said, ''I loved being the most beautiful woman, kissed by the beautiful man.''

As she became more caught up in the theatrical world, she began imitating what she saw on the screen.

Barbra spent hours in the bathroom at home, trying out various shades of make-up and creating unusual hair styles. And she visited the penny arcades near her home to take pictures of herself in different dramatic poses.

She sometimes watched TV shows on the 7½ inch screen of a neighbor family. Then she began practicing cigarette commercials in front of the bathroom mirror.

In high school Barbra met a girl who wore white make-up and ''kooky'' clothes. Attracted by this style, Barbra began rummaging through thrift shops where she bought old, long coats, fur wraps and cast-off shoes.

All of these escape routes isolated Barbra more from others her age. At Erasmus Hall High School she was a loner. The school had many tightly knit groups, and Barbra didn't fit. She has said, ''I never needed anybody really.''

But perhaps she always realized this was a defense against her hidden loneliness. Years later she was to sing a song called ''People.'' The lyrics say, ''People who need people are the luckiest people in the world.'' Barbra's own experience certainly helped her sing the song with understanding.

Barbra's first trip out of Brooklyn was an important one. At fourteen she went to Manhattan to see a stage play, *The Diary of Anne Frank*. As a result of that experience she knew she wanted to become a star. "I remember thinking that I could go up on the stage and play any role without any trouble at all," she has said.

In spite of her goal to become an actress, she would not participate in any school productions. She knew she wanted to act professionally and saw no need to spend time with amateurs.

Her choice was to find ways to become connected with the theater. She spent one summer in upstate New York, working with a group presenting plays. She didn't have much chance to act, but she changed sets, cleaned toilets, and appeared on stage briefly. She also took jobs ushering in Broadway theaters.

When Barbra graduated from high school in 1959, she was ready to leave Brooklyn, which she has often called the home of "baseball, boredom, and bad breath."

Barbra's mother disliked her daughter's idea of becoming an actress. She told Barbra she wasn't pretty enough; she was too skinny. She tried to encourage Barbra to take courses in typing and shorthand so she could get a secretarial job. But Barbra refused. She was afraid that if she had those skills, she might settle for such a job. She was determined to pursue her dream.

After leaving home, Barbra shared an apartment in Manhattan with a friend. During that time she took acting lessons from two teachers. Because she didn't want either teacher to know she had another instructor, she searched the New York phone book and selected the name "Angelina Scarangella" to use with one of the teachers.

Barbra's ambition was to be a serious actress. She wanted to perform in Shakespearian plays. Her instructors soon realized that she had a natural ability as a comedienne and tried to convince her to use that talent. But Barbra, independent as ever, fought that.

Finding a job as an actress wasn't easy. Barbra worked at small jobs to support herself while she looked. Eventually, she gave up the apartment and began carrying a portable cot with her. She'd sleep wherever she could find a place — with friends, in the loft of a theater, in a public relations office.

She still wore her "kooky" thrift shop clothes and white make-up. Her strange appearance sometimes turned off producers immediately. They wouldn't even let her try out for a part. She'd warn them, "Look, you'd better sign me up, I'm terrific." But they said she needed experience.

Friends, trying to help her, advised her to tone down her clothes, fix her Jewish nose, or change her name. Her brother Sheldon saw the rips in the back of her stockings and offered to buy her a new pair. But Barbra told him, "they're not ripped in front, and I don't see them in back; so they don't bother me." Since she wouldn't change, he made her walk three feet behind him when they were together.

The only change Barbra consented to was the spelling of her first name. She dropped the one "a" from Barbara. She refused to alter the name any more because, as she once said, "I wanted all the people I knew when I was younger to know it was me when I became a star." For even though she was often discouraged, insecure, and afraid, Barbra knew, somehow, she would be a star. As she told reporters later, "I had to be a star because my mouth is too big. I'm too whatever I am to end up in the middle."

Finally, in 1961, broke and discouraged, Barbra decided to enter a talent contest sponsored by the Lion, a Greenwich Village bar and restaurant. She entered as a singer. The only singing she had done was on the steps of her apartment building as a child. But the prize was an engagement at the bar and free suppers. "That's all I had to hear," she recalled, "and I decided to enter. I've made many a deal based on a meal."

Barbra chose to sing a ballad, "A Sleepin' Bee." Before the contest she asked some friends to listen to her but was embarrassed to perform for them. She had them face the wall while she sang. "When I finished and turned around, I remember I couldn't understand why they had tears in their eyes," she said later.

She won the contest. And that was the first major step in realizing her dream. The audiences at the Lion were fascinated by this girl with the unusual voice, strange appearance, and unique songs. In addition to her moving ballads she sang children's songs such as "Who's Afraid of the Big, Bad Wolf," and amusing tunes like "Come to the Supermarket in Old Peking." Her sense of humor permeated her acts. In her Brooklyn accent she poked fun at herself, her background, her life-style.

Following her engagement at the Lion, she appeared at the Bon Soir, another Greenwich Village nightclub. She made her debut wearing a $4 black dress, a $2 Persian vest, and old white satin shoes with silver buckles. Barbra remembers that her mother came to hear her on the second night. When she saw Barbra wearing a white lace jacket from 1890, she thought she was wearing a night-gown. But "to me it was beautiful," Barbra has related.

Even more beautiful was the happiness Barbra was beginning to experience. She has said, ". . . in life I felt that people didn't pay attention to me . . . On stage, singing, I could say what I felt; and I was listened to."

It was at the Bon Soir that Barbra met Marty Erlichman. He was impressed with her and offered to act as her agent. He has continued to represent her since then.

After eleven weeks at the Bon Soir, Barbra was accepted for a part in an off-Broadway musical revue, *Another Evening with Harry Stoones.* But the show lasted only one evening. It received poor reviews and closed due to lack of funds.

By that time, however, Barbra had already made an impression through her nightclub acts and her TV appearances. In 1961 she appeared on *The Jack Paar Show,* Mike Wallace's *PM East,* and *The David Susskind Show.* She kept her image alive wearing fur stoles, dangling jewelry, and fishnet stockings. Mert Koplin, who was then the producer of *PM East,* remembers, "She wore a simple little basic burlap bag." Barbra has admitted, "It was a big, defensive, rebellious thing. But at the same time it was theatrically *right for me I knew.*"

Late in 1961 she began an engagement at the Blue Angel — a nightclub which producers and directors often visited to discover new talent. One evening the discovery was Barbra. David Merrick was ready to produce a Broadway musical, *I Can Get It For You Wholesale.* When he heard Barbra, he knew she would be perfect for the part of Miss Marmelstein.

Barbra's playing of this role in the Broadway musical was the beginning of a career which has been astonishing in its intensity and diversity.

16

Barbra spent 1963 touring major nightclubs across the country. She also recorded her first three LP's. The first one, *The Barbra Streisand Album,* won Barbra her first Grammy for "Best Album of the Year."

In 1964 Barbra was busy starring in the Broadway musical, *Funny Girl.* Eight times a week for nearly two years, she played the role of Fanny Brice, a major star of the early 1900's. The play received rave reviews and drew large audiences. The reason was Barbra. *Cue* magazine said, "Magnificent, sublime, radiant, extraordinary, electric — what puny little adjectives to describe Barbra Streisand."

In 1965 Barbra signed a contract with CBS for $5 million agreeing to do several TV specials over a ten year period.

The following year she played *Funny Girl* in London. In 1967 Barbra turned to Hollywood to break into movies. Her first film, *Funny Girl,* was released in 1968 and won her an Oscar as "Best Actress."

Thus went Barbra's whirlwind career as she continued making films, recording albums, and doing occasional concerts.

By 1975, no one questioned Barbra's claim to stardom. She was the first person to have won Broadway's Tony, the recording industry's Grammy, television's Emmy, the movie industry's Oscar, and the International Golden Globe.

The depressing days of boring Brooklyn were gone forever. Fantasy had become reality.

Barbra's fairytale-like rise to fame even had a fairy-tale-like romance.

At the audition for *I Can Get It For You Wholesale,* Barbra appeared with two inch finger nails and purple lipstick. She sang her number and then began handing out cards with her phone number, begging anyone to call her. She had her first telephone and wanted to hear it ring.

That night she did receive a call. It was from Elliot Gould, who was to play the male lead in *Wholesale.* ''You asked for someone to call you, so I called. I just want to tell you, you were brilliant today.''

Elliot later admitted that when he first saw Barbra, he thought ''she was the weirdo of all times.'' But the more he saw her, the more he realized that she was a sensitive, love-starved person. He was shy himself and recognized Barbra's similar disposition. Later he told interviewers, ''She's fragile and exquisite. She needs taking care of. She liked me, and I think I was the first person to like her back.''

The relationship progressed rapidly. Soon Elliot was wiping out the years of loneliness Barbra had experienced.

As *Wholesale* continued, Barbra and Elliot were together almost constantly. After the show they would walk around New York, going to horror movies or playing pokerino in the penny arcades. Their relationship was very private. They spent most of their time with each other exclusively. Neither cared for large gatherings or parties.

In Barbra's apartment they spent hours playing games of checkers, cards, chess, and Monopoly. They made plans for the future. Barbra wanted them to study

Greek or Latin so they "could speak a secret language nobody else could understand."

The apartment was located on Third Avenue above a fish restaurant. The smells of the restaurant permeated the building. Elliot remembers, "We used to eat on the sewing machine. A big rat named Oscar lived in the kitchen."

But Barbra didn't care. At last she had a place where she felt she belonged and someone who cared for her.

Barbra and Elliot were married in 1963. They seemed aware of the problems they would face. Each was launching a show business career which would demand long hours of work and periods of separation. They realized that they would have difficulties, with reporters, fans, and gossip columnists constantly examining their lives.

At one point Elliot commented, "I know the traps, I know the wounds, and I've decided it's worth it to wage the battle. Our battle is especially difficult because we're real people, not just two beautiful magazine covers. We really love one another."

After their marriage, Barbra and Elliot moved into an apartment very different from the one above the fish restaurant. But even in the duplex penthouse in Manhattan, their lives expressed their unique personalities. They continued to collect old and unusual furniture, including a prized 300-year-old bed.

They also continued to eat their favorite foods, TV chicken dinners, and Barbra's favorite, coffee ice cream bricks. In 1964 Elliot talked about installing a refrigerator in the bedroom so Barbra could eat ice cream and watch TV horror movies in bed.

A most important event for Elliot and Barbra was the birth of their son Jason on December 29, 1966. For Barbra, having a child was part of the impossible dream of her childhood. She once said of herself as a child, "I would try to imagine my future, like other kids, but I couldn't; it just stopped. There was a big blank screen, no husband, no children, nothing."

So she was proud and thrilled with having a child of her own. Shortly after his birth she told an interviewer, "I take pictures every Thursday on his birthday."

After Jason's birth, Barbra hired a nurse and continued to work. But she tried to feed and bathe him as often as she could. Frequently she took him with her. While she was filming *Funny Girl,* he slept in her dressing room while she worked. Between shootings, she would feed him, carry him around, and talk to him, still concentrating on the movie.

But despite the happiness Jason brought Barbra and Elliot, the fairytale-like romance didn't have a happy-ever-after ending. The relationship they both thought was so special didn't survive. In 1969 they tried a separation. In 1971 they were divorced. Apparently, neither Barbra nor Elliot felt bitter. Barbra has said, "Once you have loved someone, he becomes a part of what you were and therefore part of what you are."

By this time Barbra was well known, and rumors often circulated about her romances. Recently the major man in her life is Jon Peters. Barbra and Jon have talked publicly about working on films together in the future. Barbra's words about Jon give the impression that he is playing an important part in her life. She has admitted that he has helped her discover what is really important to her. As she says, "His energy, enthusiasm, and ideas have given me a new excitement in my work and in my life."

"A skinny flibbertigibbet with no discipline and no technique. All she had was this enormous talent." That is producer David Merrick's recollection of Barbra when he first heard her sing in 1961.

The Singer

Her enormous talent involves a voice that can be loud and gutsy one moment and soft and sentimental the next. Barbra can sing a comic "Marty the Martian" and then awe her listeners with the dreamy sounds of "The Way We Were."

She has often called herself an actress who sings. Thinking of each song as a kind of play, Barbra works out her interpretation and then tries to convey that to the audience.

"Cry Me a River" is an example of this technique. She has said that when she originally sang the song, she had a particular person in mind. "I tried to re-create in my mind the details of his face," she admits.

Another example is her interpretation of "Happy Days Are Here Again." The song had been the fast, up-beat theme song of the Democratic Party for years. But when Barbra sings it in a very slow tempo, the words take on a new significance.

Although she works out a basic interpretation of a song, she maintains that each performance is different, influenced by the situation and her feelings at the moment.

She recalls that when she was in *Wholesale,* the directors complained that she didn't use the same gestures in every performance. "I told them, 'Just give me the music and I'll make it work every time,' and I did, and then they let me alone."

Barbra has spent time analyzing a performer's relationship to the audience. She thinks a performer can give most to the audience by total involvement in the performance. She has said, "When I sing, I go inside myself."

She has commented, too, "I also don't like to spell out everything so completely; I want the people in the audience to participate, to use their imagination, to relate the songs to their own lives. In other words, I hold back the tears so that the audience can cry."

In treating her songs this way Barbra is emotionally involved herself. Some critics have found this to be her weak point. They contend she is too intense, that she works for overstatement. Some think her style is too dynamic for the popular songs she sings. They think she might do better with opera.

People closest to Barbra think her personal involvement is what makes her appealing. Her manager, Marty Erlichman, attributes her success to the fact that people can identify with her.

He has said, "Barbra is the girl the guys never look at twice; and when she sings about that, about being like an invisible woman, people break their necks trying to protect her."

Another friend of Barbra's also feels she communicates something of herself through her songs. "She's telling you the story of her life every time she gets up there. And the facts of that life have made her very sensitive."

From the beginning of her career, Barbra has had an instinctive sense of what is right for her. She can tell if a background instrument is too loud, if she has sung a note slightly off-key, if a shot should be from a different angle. Her precision has sometimes infuriated producers and directors. But Barbra has been insistent, even if it meant redoing a song or scene many times. She once said, "If something has got to be, I can do it. Like, if the high note is right for the song, I can reach it, because that's the way it's got to be. There's always the way it's got to be."

24

Barbra has been compared to many other singers. She sounds a little like Judy Garland, Fanny Brice, Ethel Merman, Joni Mitchell, and Aretha Franklin. But mostly she sounds like the unique individual she is, Barbra Streisand, a singer with enormous talent.

The Individual

"I often think of Barbra as 46 going on 8," Elliot Gould once said.

This description seems to capture something of Barbra's personality. She is an exciting person who has many interests and ideas which are constantly changing as she lives through new experiences.

One of her long-time interests has been antiques. She once acknowledged that she liked old things "because they have proven their immortality. They know something I don't." She has collected many items over the years, usually searching for a bargain.

But in 1974 when Barbra was featured in *House Beautiful,* she said that she was no longer interested in collecting. "I really don't care for possessions now — I find them an obligation, and not necessary to my emotional health."

What she has accumulated, however, fills her 50-year-old California home and includes some very valuable and unusual art pieces and furnishings. Once she found a carpet pattern she liked in a hotel and then had one woven in Ireland in colors she chose. Another unusual item in her living room is a carved wooden horseshoe bar which came from a turn-of-the-century railroad car.

Barbra's collections include a number of Coca-Cola serving trays from the 1920's and 1930's. When Barbra began the collection, they cost $2 or $3 each; today they are valued at $100 each. She also has a collection of perfume bottles and one of the Victorian fans which are on display in her home.

In addition to valuable pieces, Barbra decorates her home with things she has found in garages and with souvenirs from the sets of her films.

Barbra's individuality has also been expressed in her choice of clothes. Her thrift shop costumes, which identified her at the beginning of her career, were eventually discarded. In 1966 she was elected to the International Best Dressed List. During the period when she was interested in extremely stylish clothes, she was featured in *Vogue* several times. She even designed some of her clothes. Critics said she had "extraordinary individuality and infallible fashion instinct."

But by 1974 she had changed her type of clothes again. She explains, "I went through a period of loving status things. Now I just wear T-shirts and dungarees and drive a Cougar. It's as if I've taken up where I left off at 18 — back to my thrift shop goodies."

Barbra is enthusiastic about certain kinds of food, too. Once she and Elliot drove around New York after a late party, looking for a place which served one of her favorite foods, rice pudding without raisins. Barbra was dressed in furs and diamonds, but was quite happy to eat in a Waterfront diner.

She claims her favorite breakfast consists of baked potatoes with sour cream and caviar. And she especially likes potatoes baked one day and reheated two days later when they are "hard on the outside and mooshy on the inside."

She has even mentioned that she's thought of running a restaurant "with barber chairs, so that in between courses you can lie back and relax — maybe have a shave or a manicure."

Only a lack of time keeps her from doing many of the new things she'd like to try. As she once said, "What I'd like is more time — time not only to read the stacks of political journals that have been piling up, but also time to read *Good Housekeeping* in order to find out different ways to decorate my son's sandwiches."

In Search of Self

"Everybody knew Barbra Streisand would be a star, and so she is," Walter Kerr wrote after the opening night of *Funny Girl* on Broadway in 1964.

Perhaps everyone knew Barbra was a star except Barbra. She had always dreamed of being famous, but it took her years to accept the fact that she had made it.

The insecurity of her childhood was difficult to overcome. On her 22nd birthday she was doing a Broadway performance of *Funny Girl.* At the curtain call a fan shouted, "Happy Birthday!" Then the whole audience took up the cry. Everyone stood up and cheered. Afterwards Barbra wondered, "What does it mean when people applaud? I don't know how to respond. Should I give 'em money? Say thank you?"

Barbra constantly looked for proof that she really was successful. When recording or rehearsing for a show, she often demanded a response from a director or producer. "All right, what is it? Am I great, or am I lousy, huh? I need to know."

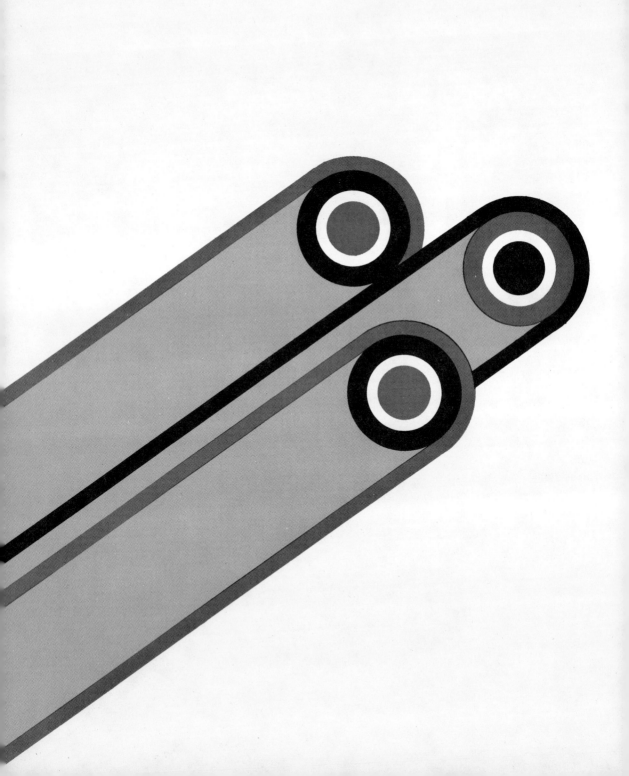

If she heard another performer sing one of her songs, she worried that it was better than her own. Once, when an understudy took her part in *Funny Girl,* she thought she'd lose her job.

In 1966 she told an interviewer, "I win awards and everything, but one of these days something is going to bomb. It's a scary thing. It can all suddenly fall apart."

As a result, she pushed herself, constantly striving for perfection in whatever she attempted. She demanded retakes of scenes in movies, retapes of recordings. Once, while on vacation in Europe, she spoke to her manager Marty Erlichman about a slight variation in pitch in a song she had recorded. He explained that only a handful of people in the world would be capable of noticing it. Her response was immediate. "That's enough. I'll do it over."

The old taunt that she was not pretty remained with her for years, too. She worried when a person would not look at her directly because she imagined that the person couldn't stand to look at her.

By 1970 she was overcoming some of her fears and insecurity. She told a *Vogue* writer, "I always felt I had to prove myself. I'm a person now. I relish my vulnerability, but I don't have this need to work. Like I don't *need* to please my mother anymore."

In 1974, thirteen years after her career was really underway, she spoke about her feelings. She seemed more relaxed with herself, more ready to deal with the question of identity. In analyzing her film, *Funny Lady,* a sequel to *Funny Girl,* she said, "The script is about really learning to accept yourself. That's what I've started doing in my own personal life."

So perhaps Barbra is finally ready to admit what everyone else has known for years. She is a star.

JACKSON FIVE
CARLY SIMON
BOB DYLAN
JOHN DENVER
THE BEATLES
ELVIS PRESLEY
JOHNNY CASH
CHARLEY PRIDE
ARETHA FRANKLIN
ROBERTA FLACK
STEVIE WONDER

NEIL DIAMOND
CAROLE KING
DIANA ROSS
THE OSMONDS
CHARLIE RICH
ELTON JOHN
CHICAGO
FRANK SINATRA
BARBRA STREISAND
OLIVIA NEWTON-JOHN

Rock'n
PopStars